Selected Poems

Paul Farley was born in Liverpool in 1965 and studied at the Chelsea School of Art. He has published four collections of poetry with Picador, most recently *The Dark Film* (2012). A frequent broadcaster, he has received numerous awards including *Sunday Times* Young Writer of the Year, the Whitbread Poetry Prize and the E. M. Forster Award from the American Academy of Arts and Letters.

Also by Paul Farley in Picador

The Dark Film

Tramp in Flames

The Ice Age

The Boy from the Chemist is Here to See You

Paul Farley

Selected Poems

PICADOR

First published 2014 by Picador
an imprint of Pan Macmillan, a division of Macmillan Publishers Limited
Pan Macmillan, 20 New Wharf Road, London N1 9RR
Basingstoke and Oxford
Associated companies throughout the world
www.panmacmillan.com

ISBN 978-1-4472-2042-8

1 3 5 7 9 8 6 4 2

A CIP catalogue record for this book is available from the British Library.

Printed and bound by CPI Group (UK) Ltd, Croydon, CR0 4YY

For Carole Romaya

Contents

FROM

The Boy from the Chemist is Here to See You

(1998)

Eaux d'Artifice

The moon we know from dreams or celluloid
is high tonight. A dried-up fountain bed
gawps back, a baroque radio telescope
the race has left behind, always on the up,
defying gravity. The park seems of an age
that tried, in other small ways, to oblige
the same imperative – this domed palm-house
that brought the sky down closer; these dark yews
clipped conically and pointed heavenwards;
and fountains that suspended arcs and cords
of water, one so powerful it could hold
the weight of terrified cats or 'a Small Childe'
in its jets. The water only comes here now
to rest after the dream-days spent in cloud,
to swill round with the leaves and empty cans,
and then moves on. Its work is never done,
like man's, a thought that brings me back to earth:
soaked through with sweat, under her bone-light,
bouncing my signals back and forth all night,
the moon drowns out a point low in the south
that could be Mercury or the Eutalsat,
though these days she in turn has to compete
with our restless nightside. When I can't sleep
I walk these rhododendroned paths that keep
to strict ideas of sunset and sunrise,
and find my level on a bench, like this.

Depot

You wouldn't know a place like this existed.
It shows the street its modest, oily features
(a door I walked right past on my first day),
but opens into hangar-like proportions.
Here are the bays where dustcarts spend their evenings,
where grit summers, dreaming of Januaries,
and barriers mesh like deckchairs off-season.

I've dreamt of something like this sorting-house,
and walked its film-set streets, and tried its swings
some nights – the perfect playground, deserted –
but didn't know a place like this existed;
that crippled boys who stood outside our chemists
would form ranks like a terracotta army
in lives beyond thalidomide and weather.

Was this what lay behind the knowing winks
I caught between binmen, or am I dreaming
that road sweepers held doctorates in philosophy;
and knew, after the miles behind a big broom,
they would return to worlds not unlike this one,
find a spotless bench, and read their *Echo*
in the irony of strip lights over street lamps.

Termini

We lived where buses turned back on themselves,
when drivers still referred to us as 'scholars',
winding on their final destination
and we would end up here: PIER HEAD.
Today, a spinning blade blows surf 'n' turf
from a steakhouse kitchen, luring those
with appetites sharpened by river air
after a windswept round trip on the ferry.
What else is there? The city has shrunk back
from the front, slowly, over the years
leaving this airy strand the buses bypass,
and now nobody's journey into town
ends with a top-deck, front-seat panorama.
I left the slashed seat and the listing bottle
to finish this journey on foot, in the rain,
the same route where the brothers Lumière
cranked the first nitrate from a moving train;
and stand now where we sagged the long school day
eating hot dogs, watching buses turn
back to the far estates with lower case names,
an audience staying put for the minor credits.

Electricity

It comes as a shock to that first audience.
The street they walked in off just moments before
hangs pale on the wall. All the colour has gone,
and its faces and carriages have ground to a blur.

Remember, no one has thought of pianos
or credits. The performance will start off mid-scene,
once each hard bench is filled, when the first usher nods
and the lamp is turned up and the crank starts to turn

and their hairs stand on end to a shimmer of leaves
or the movement of clouds, and the way that the tense
has been thrown like a switch, where the land turns to dreams,
and where, sad to say, we have been living since.

A Thousand Hours

There were false starts, but life, for me, really
began the night he unplugged the telly
and snuffed the pilot light. As last-man-out
he worked right through to dawn, between the street
and this bedroom, until he'd stripped it bare,
but left me in his rush to check the meter,
to turn the stopcock on a copper tank,
count stairs and memorize that manhole's clunk,
the first hawked phlegm, the way a window pane
was answering the early Lime Street train;
and posted back his keys to nobody.

I've hung here naked since, by day barely
able to force a shadow to be thrown.
It's nights I come into my own:
a halo for the ceiling, corners for mice,
and through the glass a phantom of all this,
a twin star that is shedding kilowatts
in translation. Beyond these dark outskirts
my creator sleeps. I recall how his eyes
would whirr just like this night-time visitor
that might outlive me. Of all his ideas
I burn on, having been conceived in error.

Laws of Gravity

(for Julian Turner)

I found a guidebook to the port he knew
intimately – its guano-coated ledges,
its weathervanes, his bird's-eye river view
of liner funnels, coal sloops and dredgers.
It helped me gain a foothold – how he felt
a hundred rungs above a fifties street,
and whether, being so high, he ever dwelt
on suicide, or flummoxed his feet
to last night's dance steps, still fresh in his head.
It's all here in his ledger's marginalia:
how he fell up the dark stairwell to bed
and projected right through to Australia;
and said a prayer for rainfall every night
so he could skip his first hungovered round.
The dates he's noted *chamois frozen tight*
into bucket. When he left the ground
a sense of purpose overtook and let
a different set of laws come into play:
like muezzins who ascend a minaret
to call the faithful of a town to pray.
Take one step at a time. Never look down.
He'd seen the hardest cases freeze halfway,
the arse-flap of their overalls turn brown.
As a rule, he writes, *your sense of angle*
becomes acute at height. A diagram

he's thumbnailed shows a drop through a triangle
if you miscalculated by a gram.
Sometimes, his senses still blunted from booze,
he'd drop his squeegee, watch it fall to earth
and cling onto the grim hypotenuse
of his own making for all he was worth.
He seems to have enjoyed working that hour
the low sun caught the glass and raised the ante
on every aerial, flue and cooling tower,
and gilded the lofts, the rooftop shanty
town, when everything was full of itself,
and for a while even the Latin plaques
ignited with the glow of squandered wealth.
At times like these I see what our world lacks,
the light of heaven on what we've produced
and here some words lost where his biro bled
then *clouds of dark birds zero in to roost.*
There's IOUs and debtors marked in red
and some description of the things he saw
beyond the pane – a hard-lit typing pool,
a room of faces on some vanished floor
closed off and absolute like a fixed rule.
His story of the boy butting a wall,
the secretary crying at her desk,
all happened in the air above a mall.
Each edifice, each gargoyle and grotesque,
is gone. The earliest thing I remember:
as our van dropped a gear up Brownlow Hill
I looked back at the panes of distemper
that sealed a world. We reached our overspill,

and this is where our stories overlap.
The coming of the cradle and sheet glass
was squeezing out the ladder and the slap
of leather into suds, and less and less
work came through the door. And anyway
you were getting too old for scaling heights.
Now, when I change a bulb or queue to pay
at fairs, or when I'm checking in for flights,
I feel our difference bit down to the quick.
There are no guidebooks to that town you knew
and this attempt to build it, brick by brick,
descends the page. I'll hold the foot for you.

Era

Hide some under the carpet, line a drawer
so they will know about us, who we were
and what we did on one day years ago,
our births and deaths, our sales and tide tables.
Make a mental note of sizes no one
has seen or heard of, before it's too late –
Colombier, Imperial, Elephant –
and though the forests exhale a long sigh
of relief, what hope is there for this page
you're reading now? Cash in your mattressed wads:
they cease to be tender as of midnight.

Aquarius

More fool you who believe in the end of decades.
The seventies live on in top-floor flats
you can't see in for overgrown pot plants;
where someone struggles to crack a dial-band set
and Che stares down onto an unmade bed.

Letters pile up, shoring the front door
like a drift. Mung shoots replenish themselves
and the tap water's good for ages yet.
They never leave the room or check the view.
The neighbours wonder, as they come and go,

at such bad taste in music and curtains;
but eventually come to admire such cool retro.
Behind closed doors there is low talk of scurvy
as they carve a dice from the dwindling oatcake
cast years ago inside a chest of drawers.

After they tune out their hair will grow, for a while,
and the plants will still pull to the sun, until
the soil cracks and dries. Then, and only then,
will the old decade die, and your amazing nineties
shed its light; its seen-it-all-before light.

Treacle

Funny to think you can still buy it now,
a throwback, like shoe polish or the sardine key.
When you lever the lid it opens with a sigh
and you're face-to-face with history.
By that I mean the unstable pitch black
you're careful not to spill, like mercury

that doesn't give any reflection back,
that gets between the cracks of everything
and holds together the sandstone and bricks
of our museums and art galleries;
and though those selfsame buildings stand
hosed clean now of all their gunk and soot,

feel the weight of this tin in your hand,
read its endorsement from one Abram Lyle
'Out of the strong came forth sweetness'
below the weird logo of bees in swarm
like a halo over the lion carcass.
Breathe its scent, something lost from our streets

like horseshit or coalsmoke; its base note
a building block as biblical as honey,
the last dregs of an empire's dark sump;
see how a spoonful won't let go of its past,
what the tin calls back to the mean of its lip
as you pour its contents over yourself

and smear it into every orifice.
You're history now, a captive explorer
staked out for the insects; you're tarred
and feel its caul harden. The restorer
will tap your details back out of the dark:
close-in work with a toffee hammer.

Dependants

How good we are for each other, walking through
a land of silence and darkness. You
open doors for me, I answer the phone for you.

I play jungle loud. You read with the light on.
Beautiful. The curve of your cheekbone,
explosive vowels, exact use of cologne.

What are you thinking? I ask in a language of touch
unique to us. You tap my palm *nothing much.*
At stations we compete senses, see which

comes first – light in the tunnel, whiplash down the rail.
I kick your shins when we go out for meals.
You dab my lips. I finger yours like Braille.

Monopoly

We sat like slum landlords around the board
buying each other out with fake banknotes,
until we lost more than we could afford,
or ever hope to pay back. Now our seats
are empty – one by one we left the game
to play for real, at first completely lost
in this other world, its building sites, its rain;
but slowly learned the rules or made our own,
stayed out of jail and kept our noses clean.
And now there's only me – sole freeholder
of every empty office space in town,
and from the quayside I can count the cost
each low tide brings – the skeletons and rust
of boats, cars, hats, boots, iron, a terrier.

A Minute's Silence

The singing stops. Each player finds his spot
around the ten-yard circle that until
tonight seemed redundant, there just for show.
The PA asks us to observe the hush.

We find we're standing in a groundsman's shoes,
the quiet he must be familiar with
while squeaking chalk-paste up the grassy touch,
or overseeing a private ritual

and scattering the last mortal remains
of a diehard fan beneath each home-end stanchion.
No one keeps a count or checks their watch
so space is opened up. It seems to last

a small eternity – the happy hour
that stretches to three, the toast, the final spin.
I observe the silence sneak through turnstiles
and catch on quick – a bar muffles its pumps;

in function rooms, a wedding reception
freezes still as its own photograph;
an awful bagwash winds down mid-cycle –
a Saturday gridlocked, unaccompanied

by hooters or sirens. Like early audiences
we have left the street to its own devices
to watch the flicking shadow of itself
onscreen, the purring spool somehow apart

from all of this. It leaves the one-way system
and finds less work to do outside of town:
a rookery, light aircraft, and the wind
banging gates or moaning through the lines.

(How still without birdsong. It still guts me
to think of all the havoc wreaked each spring
we combed the hedges outside our estate
and stole the still-warm clutches from each nest;

all that music, blown and set in file
on sawdust in a two-pound biscuit tin,
displayed to rivals in attack formation,
a 4-3-3 of fowls and passerines.)

Sooner or later silence reaches the coast
and stops just short of getting its feet wet.
There's something of the Ice Age to all this.
The only sound's the white noise of the sea

that is all song, all talk, all colour, mixed.
Before that whistle bursts a hole and brings
the air rushing back in with arc lighting,
calls for owners of the double parked,

the last verse of 'You'll Never Walk Alone'
(never . . . *the sweet silver song of a lark*)
listen, to where the shore meets the salt water;
a million tiny licking, chopping sounds:

the dead, the never-born, the locked-out souls
are scratching on the thin shell we have grown
around ourselves. Listen. The afternoon
is dark already, and there is a moon.

Without Potatoes

'Without potatoes we would be like loose threads on
a loom, for potatoes are what bind life together.'
– Amarayan proverb

We took spud guns onto the terraces,
Threw King Edwards spiked with razor blades.
Ate chips salted and vinegared,
Burnt our cheeks on the polished nickel, waiting.

We danced the mashed pah-tay-tah;
Wrestled with earthy sackfuls
Dropped from chutes on childhood errands;
Watched the roasty fall from ubiquity
On Sundays centred round gas ovens
To french fries, Spud-U-Like and waffles.

I miss the simple pleasures – of rinsing
A tuber under a cold tap; of coiling the peelings
Into a bucket; of gouging the eyes out.
I never thought I'd come to say such things.

Documentarist

It's clear I love the footage of the past:
its herring catches, silvery flinders
that flap in unimagined elements,
the miner's face that bares bright teeth and eyes
to camera, the skies scribbled and crossed
by a century's dust. A cold, unglamorous

photography no starlet or leading man
could feel at home for long in. Peeling walls,
five to a bed . . . See how they're smiling still
from deep inside their mould-invaded tins –
a porterage through equatorial damp,
incisors flared. Look back into this lens

beyond the here-and-now, to darkened rooms:
the future screens its ideas of us,
to rows that multiply back endlessly.
Smile, as they file out to a world
of worked-out seams, depopulated seas,
the ancient shock of daylight still playing.

Keith Chegwin as Fleance

The next rung up from extra and dogsbody
and all the clichés are true – days waiting for
enough light, learning card games, penny-ante,
while fog rolls off the sea, a camera
gets moisture in its gate, and Roman Polanski
curses the day he chose Snowdonia.

He picked you for your hair to play this role:
a look had reached Bootle from Altamont
that year. You wouldn't say you sold your soul
but learned your line inside a beating tent
by candlelight, the shingle dark as coal
behind each wave, and its slight restatement.

'A tale told by an idiot . . .' 'Not your turn,
but perhaps, with time and practice . . .', the Pole starts.
Who's to say, behind the accent and that grin,
what designs you had on playing a greater part?
The crew get ready while the stars go in.
You speak the words you'd written on your heart

just as the long-awaited sunrise fires
the sky a blueish pink. Who could have seen
this future in the late schedules, where I
can't sleep, and watch your flight from the big screen;
on the other side of drink and wondering why,
the zany, household-name years in between?

Not Fade Away

A cornfield deep in drifts. I walked an hour
without moving. The outskirts of a town
that felt, with all its ploughed streets and neon,
like stepping from a page. I found a bar
and tried to force a boilermaker down.
The barman asked if I was twenty-one.

You don't crawl free from crashes every day.
In celebration of that windchilled night
I've pissed the intervening years away
in dark corners, doorways, and come so far
from all those screaming girls, the cold limelight
winks back faint as a star.

No one believes the bore who doesn't wash
or listens to the stories he lets slip
while stoking the jukebox. Nobody looks
twice at the guy being given the bum's rush;
my legend melts down to a tiny blip,
a half-tone dot on album sleeves, in books.

I retrace my own trail and wipe it dead.
The scene is how I left it. Carefully
I ease myself back down among the wreck's
ice-dusted cache – the dials the crew misread,
the Bopper's dice and Ritchie's crucifix –
and wait for history.

The Sleep Of Estates

In living rooms where fathers sprawl, still clothed,
the bumpy core beyond Sinatra's voice
beats inside a radiogram, a pulse
deep under. There's rain on the windows.

The last buses have left their termini,
each destination cranked to a blank stare.
The grilles that scented underpass and square
have wound down now after the final fry.

The hour belongs to slamming taxi doors,
the clack of heels and laughter in the night;
while mothers wait for clubs to empty out
and faulty street lighting blinks out a morse

that no bare-legged curfew breaker reads.
Young addresses dream of being listed,
double-glazed, damp-coursed, sandblasted,
and rid of roosting seabirds. Overhead

the air is rich with night-time radio,
with baby-listeners, and coded words
that leak from patrol cars and amateurs
across backlanes where cab drivers won't go.

The door shuts soft. The rain has turned to ice.
She lifts the arm out of infinity
in Huyton, and in Skem and Speke and Stockie
née Cantril Farm, so good they named it twice.

Stray

Whatever brought me to the gutter
had something to do with this:
a tree-lined journey to the shop for booze,
paracetamol and papers
where I came across his name
on a photocopied flyer
tacked to the bark of every other trunk.
I soon got to know his sooty coat,
reflective collar. So tenderly written
I half-expected a *Last seen wearing* . . .

Someone had added *Try the Peking Garden*
in shaky freehand. There was a reward
so I started to keep an eye out.
When you asked me what I was thinking
staring through a cloud of midges
those evenings we sat outside drinking
it was usually to do with him –
slowly turning to mulch in deep thicket;
eaten alive by pit bulls;
or his carbon copy, given to a child

who thought him lost to the night.
We'd take in the chairs. I'd sit in the window
listening to far-off sirens
and the sound of my breathing. He was stretching,
getting used to the name they'd given him.

It grew, until one night in September
we ran low on smokes. You sent me to the garage.
I walked down that road with the trees
heavy and still. Hardly a whisper. Turned
past the all-nighter and kept on walking.

FROM

The Ice Age

(2002)

From a Weekend First

One for the money. Arrangements in green and grey
from the window of an empty dining-car.
No takers for this Burgundy today
apart from me. I'll raise a weighted stem
to my homeland scattering by, be grateful for
these easy-on-the-eye, Army & Navy
surplus camouflage colours that seem
to mask all trace of life and industry;

a draft for the hidden dead, our forefathers,
the landfills of the mind where they turned in
with the plush and orange peel of yesteryear,
used up and entertained and put to bed
at last; to this view where everything seems to turn
on the middle distance. Crematoria, multiplex
way stations in the form of big sheds
that house their promises of goods and sex;

to the promise of a university town,
its spires and playing fields. No border guards
will board at this station, no shakedown
relieve me of papers or contraband:
this is *England*. Nobody will pull the cord
on these thoughts, though the cutlery and glasses
set for dinner are tinkling at a bend,
a carriage full of ghosts taking their places.

Now drink to slow outskirts, the colour wheels
of fifty years collected in windows;
to worlds of interiors, to credit deals
with nothing to pay until next year, postcodes
where water hardens, then softens, where rows
of streetlights become the dominant motif
as day drains, and I see myself transposed
into the dark, lifting my glass. Belief

is one thing, though the dead have none of it.
What would they make of me? This pinot noir
on my expenses, time enough to write
this on a Virgin antimacassar –
the miles of feint, the months of Sunday school,
the gallons of free milk, all led to here:
an empty dining-car, a single fool
reflected endlessly on the night air.

11th February 1963

The worst winter for decades. In the freeze
some things get lost and I'm not even born,
but think until you're many Februaries
deep in thought with me and find London
on that day as held inside a glacier;
a fissure where two postal districts touch,
its people caught mid-floe, at furniture,
the contents of their stomachs, a stopped watch.
At these pressures the distance has collapsed:
the studio clock winds up over Primrose Hill,
or the poet and her sleeping children crossed
the mile to Abbey Road. This milk bottle
might hold what John'll drink for one last take;
that she'll leave out for when the children wake.

Big Safe Themes

You can look all you like but the big safe themes are there
all around, forestalling what you were going to say.
A robust description of a cedarwood cigar box
has grown so big it could now contain Cuba and history.

No refuge in things. They stand at one or two removes
from the big themes; so any warm-weather fruit might bring
visiting times and the loved one we begged not to leave
as soon as you sniff at the rind or spit out a pip.

You can start with a washer, a throat lozenge, a mouse-mat
and watch them move in like the weather. Trying to be brave
ends in tears: I've seen the big safe themes walk all over
incest and morris dancing in their ten-league boots.

Why resist anyway? Bend with the big safe themes.
Let them do what they will and admit that the road you walk
again and again – right down to its screw-thread of blood
in a quivering phlegm – is becoming your big safe theme.

Cod

Those deep-sea fish had claims upon our souls.
What held the sense of mystery in our lives
like dark Good Fridays? Sometimes, if the rain
had slickened the streets into a Stanhope Forbes
and turned sandstone to pewter; if the forecast
gave more rain from the west for days on end
and warnings to the various fishing grounds,
we'd feel them close, a nuzzling all around,
the brush of barbels on causeways and piers,
their sea lanes washing into B-roads;
and, huddling in around our radios,
we'd trawl the bandwidths for a sign that soon
the sheet of cloud would break, the fish recede
back to the ocean cold from whence they came.

The Ages

The trees lay down their seam of coal as thin
as hammered gold leaf all afternoon
when a child is called in from the Iron Age war
he's been waging with the next street; road-works reach
the water table by teatime then knock off
for the day; late sun catches the last post
being emptied from an Edwardian pillar box,
warms the sleeping sandstone in its vertical dream;
there is a low Vent-Axian hum round the backs
of buildings, the usual insect holocaust
on filaments and coils; that hardening of the heart
that steals up on us like an early frost.

The ages, coming thick and fast tonight.
I caught one on my bedroom ceiling: the globe
of a paper light-shade caught in headlights
was a Golden Age symbol of truth and reason;
then a cold planet again. I yawn and fear the dark
like any good caveman. The buzzing that disturbs
my sleep might be a moth, or just the Creation
doing its thing on the skyline. I lie awake
in the blue chill, listening to the last teenagers
passing the house, their cries in the ever-after.

Dead Fish

Remember how they made us play Dead Fish?
If it rained, the dinner-ladies kept us in
and we cleared the canteen of its chairs and tables.
Have you forgotten how we lay so still?
The smell of old varnish, salt on the parquet,
or how the first five minutes were the easiest?
You'd find an attitude that you were sure
could last until the bell. Foetal, recovery:
each had his favourite. I'd strike a simple
flat-on-back, arms-by-my-sides figure
and concentrate.

Some fell asleep,
easy after seconds of tapioca,
and this proved fatal. Sleep is seldom still.
Others could last as long as pins and needles
allowed, or until they couldn't frame
the energies of being six years old:
some thought would find its way into a limb
and give the game away. But you were good,
so good you always won, so never saw
this lunch-time slaughter of the innocents
from where we sat out on the bean-bagged margin.
Dead fish in uniform, oblivious
to dinner-ladies' sticks poking their ribs,
still wash up on my mind's floor when it rains
in school hours. Blink if you remember this.

Establishing Shot

It might as well come here as anywhere.
Pick any card: street-lamps, tall leylandii,
rotated ryegrass in available light.
A long, slow take. Half-closing day. No one
playing out. A goal-mouth chalked on brick
is a frame within a frame just for a moment
before the artless pan resumes: bollards
and gutter-grass; and those who've just dipped in
expecting wide-screen, a lone rider
descending from high plains; the sans serifs
of Hollywood, strong language from the outset
or a director's trademark opening
will want their money back. We may as well
admit this is THE END too, while we're here.

The National in Exile

(MANOD QUARRY, NORTH WALES)

You recognise the image in the image:
in black-and-white, they stand to either side
of Jan van Eyck's 'The Arnolfini Marriage'
like any tour group taken by their guide.
But what you took to be the gallery wall
is banded with the seams of solid rock;
those men are not your classic urbanites
either: boots mark them out for dirty work
and elements; those layers that they feel
the kind of cold you find at depths or heights.

Beyond the frame a wider picture spawns:
the steep path up through shale they always took,
waist deep through each lake of moonlit ferns
to a village in some radioless nook
of a valley, where other evacuees
are sleeping in a quiet they've never known,
their eyes led through a dream of hills and distance
that they will carry back to factory towns
with their little suitcases; the schools and galleries
emptied for the blackout and insurance,

the great halls stencilled with landscapes and portraits
of wallpaper; the light of history
packed up and carried underground in crates.
The masterpieces hang here on display
in this most private of views, where slatemasons
rotate El Greco, Turner and Seurat
because no-one is looking, because the gaze
of 1941 is like a searchlight
trained on the incendiary heavens.
Each must have his favourite: the blaze

of barred coal sunsets, an avenue
of trees, the traders driven from the temple . . .
They must take it in turns to guard them through
the night, knowing these angels that people
their dark world won't return in this life;
that the slate they cut will take its own Grand Tour
into a larger, worldly exhibition
that roofs Europe. But let your eye repair
outside all that, inside this photograph,
this match of hosts with atmospheric conditions.

Joseph Beuys

To write about elemental things, to render
the world in its simpler smells and shapes and textures,
to describe how tallow collects under the finger-

nails, how felt feels against bare skin
is not, I repeat, not an option
having lived several times removed from the world as itself,

although it can do no harm to imagine
myself as the stricken airman
carted indoors by the local women

who'd take it in turns attending to the matter
of rubbing in the Stork SB and Flora,
the Golden Churn and I Can't Believe It's Not Butter.

For the House Sparrow, in Decline

Your numbers fall and it's tempting to think
you're deserting our suburbs and estates
like your cousins at Pompeii; that when you return
to bathe in dust and build your nests again
in a roofless world where no one hears your *cheeps,*
only a starling's modem mimicry
will remind you of how you once supplied
the incidental music of our lives.

A Tunnel

A tunnel, unexpected. The carriage lights
we didn't notice weren't on prove their point
and a summer's day is cancelled out, its greens
and scattered blue, forgotten in an instant

that lasts the width of a down, level to level,
a blink in *London to Brighton in Four Minutes*
that dampens mobiles – conversations end
mid-sentence, before speakers can say

'. . . a tunnel' – and the train fills with the sound
of itself, the rattle of rolling stock amplified,
and in the windows' flue a tool-shed scent,
metal on metal, a points-flash photograph,

and inside all of this a thought is clattering
in a skull inside the train inside the tunnel
inside great folds of time, like a cube of chalk
in a puncture-repair tin at a roadside

on a summer day like the one we'll re-enter
at any moment, please, at any moment.
Voices are waiting at the other end
to pick up where we left off. 'It was a tunnel . . .'

Diary Moon

You are the plainest moon. Forget all others:
shivering in pools, or spoken to when drunk,
that great Romantic gaze of youth; shed all
sonatas, harvests, Junes, and think instead
of how your phases turn here in a diary:
stripped of sunlight, surface noise and seas
you move unnoticed through the months, a bare limn
achieving ink blackness, emptying again.

You who turned inside the week-to-view
my father carried round each year, past crosses
that symbolized pay days, final demands;
in girlfriends', where red novae marked the dates
they were 'due on', and I shouldn't've been looking;
who even showed in weighty Filofaxes,
peeping through the clouds of missed appointments,
arrivals and departures, names and numbers.

On nights like these, which of us needs reminding
to set an eel-trap, open up the bomb doors
or sail out of the harbour on a spring-tide?
What sway do you hold over our affairs?
Although for some you're all that's there, printed
across the white weeks until New Year;
moving towards windows that will not frame us,
into the evenings of our sons and daughters.

The Sea in the Seventeenth Century

God's foot upon the treadle of the loom,
the sea goes about its business.
The photogenic reefs of the Pacific
can build for an eternity before
the cameras come, the kelp-forested shelves
of cooler waters absorb the wrecks
that scour their beds, a hint of the drift-net.
Ocean life goes on as usual, though.
A pulsing, absolute state of affairs
where all our yesteryears go through the lives
we might still live. It's boring in a way,
like heaven. Good Friday, 1649:
the first elvers have gained the estuaries
of Europe; a generation of spider crabs
are wiped out by a crustacean virus;
box jellyfish are deserting the shores
of a yet-to-be uncovered continent.
You'd almost think, nature being nature,
there would be some excitement at the trace
of poison from the Severn; at one part
night soil to the billionth of Thames:
that sightings of the brass-helmeted diver
would start a murmuring that God is dead.

Umbrella

I'm looking for a classical umbrella,
the kind Freud dreamt of, newly evolved
from walking-stick, before it lost its ferrule
or gained a fancy telescopic action.

I'm not interested in going so far back
as parasol or bondgrace, or lurching
sideways into Crusoe's skin and bones
contraption, or the lean-tos of antiquity.

No. I want the deeper, bat-wing pitch
that swarms and darkens streets in rainy footage;
a stick with weight and heft – hickory perhaps –
that lightens when its canopy is raised,

cut from a cloth that blocks out light as sure
as camera capes or courthouse head-blankets;
that, taut, could envelop the listener's head
and amplify the racket from a cloudburst.

Eight spokes, the heavens carved up into zones.
Italian work, the black Strad of umbrellas.
I'm still looking, soaked to the skin outside
an importer of handmade fetish wear.

Relic

One's a crown, two's a crown,
three, four, five distal occlusal,
six distal occlusal, seven occlusal.
Upper left: one mesial incisal,
two mesial incisal, three's a crown,
four, five is absent, space closed.
Six occlusal, seven occlusal, eight.
Lower left: one's a crown, two mesial,
three, four occlusal, five is absent,
space closed. Six occlusal, seven occlusal,
eight is absent. Right: one, two, three,
four distal occlusal, five's a buckle,
six and seven are absent, space closed.

Peter and the Dyke

He's in there still, with Johnny Appleseed,
with all the frogs and sleeping princesses
but won't budge. I've tempted him with liquorice,
with pipe tobacco and Dutch magazines.
This is dedication, a child's endurance.
Outside, the longshore drift of my late teens
and pull of every tide that's turned since
are as nothing to his freezing fingertip.

Negatives

Years after the chemist we hold them aloft
to see if all is right in that other world:
this sliver of a snowy strand at midnight,
its rocky outcrop molten in dark sea,
and in its lee an aunt emerging from
a black beach-towel, pupal and six years old

again. Your mother builds an ice-palace
and stares back radiantly as if her soul
is burning to escape; everyone frames
an inner light, even the men who've found
a half-decent alehouse and stand soot-faced
at a long bar of porcelain and glass,
glamorous in silver tuxedos.

We have to handle negatives carefully
the envelopes say as we slide them back
in paper frosted up like lounge-bar glass,
like ice knocked from a pond, the middle key
we sometimes find unchanged and by itself
on hot afternoons; that has no negative.

Monkfish

Fishmongers, with an eye on trade,
will usually take the head
clean off, and offer up the tail
on slopes of oily piste instead.

A waste. Eyes that have known a dark
so absolute deserve this kind
of afterlife in ours; to look
upon this kingdom of the blind.

Memento mori in Waitrose.
A skull dropped in my parka hood
by John the Grave, who terrorized
the Liverpool of my childhood.

Thorns

I saw it all sharply again at a thousand feet,
above the tree-line, my eye being drawn
away from The Lion and the Lamb, coming to rest
on the solitary black mass of a thorn
growing out of grey rock;
or my ear was led by the song-flight
of a shrike on its way to the nest:
either way I was hooked.

It looked like a mould of the veins of the heart,
a fright-wig, a land-mine under a dugout
stilled by a shutter, depending on where I stood;
it was crooked at an angle, set
firm as if in the face of a gale
even on the calmest day, in one mind, alert
should one of those 'worst blizzards
in living memory' come over the hill.

A bush fitted with its own weapon system.
I approached it the way you would
a Burryman, his arms outstretched for a burr-hug,
or a porcupine ready to draw blood.
The Biblical ur-plant, twisted to its core,
knotted and fibrous, each wizened stem
carrying code out to its furthest twig.
I'd seen the like of all of this before:

they planted thorn in the Groves and Brows and Folds
we moved out to in 1971
and it thrived, above and beyond
the caged saplings, the windbreaks of pine,
old beech shedding its mast onto concrete
and dying slowly in streetlight. Its stranglehold
was absolute and everywhere you'd find
great brakes and stands of it.

I look back on that time as into a thorn bush:
never some easy flashback,
more a tangle to be handled with due care.
Speared among the larder of the shrike
I imagined the wrappers of extant/extinct brands,
unspooled cassette tape, a cash-till cartouche,
all snagged on the hardy perennial of my childhood years.
I moved in with my hands

past a house-sparrow – a *spadger* – airlifted up
from some lowland estate
by the butcher-bird, which brought to mind
some early lore: when budgies headed straight
from their cages for open windows, to fly
out into that world, they'd manage one aerial lap
before the scrambled spadgers found
their range and locked on. From a slate-grey sky

there'd be a snowfall of bright feathers
as if angels were having a pillow-fight.
Branches fork and meet, twist and snarl
the way fiction and fact collude and clot,
drawing blood and attention.
I follow one. It leads to my grandfather,
who lived just long enough to see us go decimal
and move out twenty stops to 'that midden',

only here he's a soldier again on the Western Front
caught on one inch of the millions of kilometres of wire
that coiled through his stories: Arras, Amiens,
Ypres. A teenage Volunteer
feeling the wind turning volte-face,
and from across the salient
the first whiff of phosgene.
He pisses on a handkerchief and covers his face

and I lose his features to the twisting thorn,
mediaeval in its methods of war
and the best defence for a sleeping Ladybird princess.
I helped build such a zareba
myself once; wove thistle, bramble and nettle
to fortify and hold onto a back-field den,
to keep out the shite-hawks of Halewood, Speke and Widnes.
Helix of carpet-tacks, staples and BCG needles

I could spike pages from that world up like receipts:
The Observer's Book of Birds' Eggs,
the *Edge* westerns, Ed McBain and Sven Hassell,
the works of Herbert (Frank and James), *Street Drugs*,
The Joy of Sex I doubt anyone shared,
Papillon, with its butterfly-and-rusty-padlock conceit,
the *Pan Book of Horror* series, the Bible,
The Valley of the Dolls and *The Thorn Birds*.

I could get my wires crossed and hear my mother
whacking the ganglion that grew in her wrist
with our bible, the Freemans catalogue
or the phone book, whichever was heaviest;
could hear the air-brakes of buses bound for town,
the grudging *alright*'s between shift workers
below my window, the barking of great-grand-dogs,
and a voice I'm sure was my own:

by now, the bush had started to look
like a sprinter coming out of the blocks
or as if it were about to jump
like an angry hill god, or a Jack-from-a-box.
The blood must have drained from my face:
body-clock and mountain time seemed to be stuck,
bringing another world to life and I felt a lump
harden in my throat as the bush spoke:

Remember me? I know I'm looking rough.
It's me, you silly cunt: you if you'd stayed
back there until the bulldozers moved in.
I'm everything you might but never made
of yourself, a man stripped to his fighting weight.
I'm what you like to think you've shaken off,
though every place you've ever been since then
has seen something of me along the way.

Even here – walking in the English Lakes! –
they'll meet the prickly pear, the spiky fucker
beneath the surface, as you see me here.
The years have been cruel to you, old mucker;
turned you shite-soft, your sharp edges to mush.
See how I've still got everything it takes
to hang on, while you've drank a lake of beer
and toked so much you could turn into a bush!

All his soft tissues eaten away.
I wanted to point the finger, to blame someone,
to turn this bush into a voodoo doll
reversed out; so I could impale Lubetkin
and Luftwaffe; the faceless councillors
and aldermen who gave the nod one day
decades ago; all those I thought accountable
dangling in an aquatint by Goya.

But finding such an image of myself
in such an unlikely place
left little room for blame, and the sap
soon dropped. Surprising myself, I said to his face:
'The two of us both wanted the same thing
once. Many's the time we've taken off
out of the hardness, going way past our stop
into the sticks and breaking into song

as townee dreck tend to when on the move,
littering the sides of public roads.
It's happened here before: a girl from Manchester
left proof, a few sorry words
at the door of a two hundred years old journal;
or the discharged soldier, still seen from a grove
of 'thick hawthorn', in verse, not far from here.
Though by and large they've become invisible.

The teenage me kept shtumm, inscrutable
and bush-like again on these matters,
and a softness rose in me thinking of him
failing to make his mark, and all the others
who grew up in those unraked Zen gardens
among the bonsai thorn, the babble
of television on in the daytime;
and if this were a vision, then here it ends

with a man stood shivering at a thousand feet.
My speech is still a thorny, north-west stew;
I walk along each public right-of-way
a trespasser; there is no single view
worth taking; rootless man, still clinging on
to some idea of truth, some ideal state
just round the next bend, found out today
he's bound towards a republic of thorns,

the flag it flies: straining, grey polythene;
its rhyme and scheme, the way it founds a voice;
its bird-life, clinging to an older way;
the way it soldiers on and knows its place.
The wind picked up. And so I left the thorn
abiding there, and dropped onto the green
and soft floor of an easygoing valley,
imagining I could start from scratch again.

An Interior

They ask why I still bother coming back.
London must be great this time of year.
I'm not listening. My eyes have found
the draining-board, its dull mineral shine,
the spice rack, still exactly how I left it,
knives, a Vermeer vinyl table-mat.
How many hours did I spend watching
the woman pouring milk into a bowl
that never fills? I never tired of it.
Vision persists, doesn't admit the breaks
the artist must have taken, leg-stretching
alongside a canal twitching with sky
not unlike the leaden one outside;
or just leant on the door jamb, looking out
onto a courtyard, smoking a pipe
before going in, to sleep on his excitement.

Surtsey

Someday I'll make the trip via Icelandair
then boat to Surtsey, to stake a claim
on an island that was still active the year
I was born; a toe-hold in the North Atlantic
being photographed from planes for future terms
in distant Comprehensives. I could walk

that same dark coastline we watched thrown up
in Geography; its lava lakes, lagoons
and fountains cooled to a concrete townscape;
could spread a palm against its walls and floors
like kids who climbed the apron to feel the screen
for warmth; could catch that same trace of sulphur

we caught on a Widnes wind; could carry the words
we learned then – *magma, pumice, rivulet* –
back to source, and see how well the birds
have done since a pair of gulls in sixty-eight;
or how a cruciform of sea rocket
has bloomed beyond the classroom's colour plates

and flourished like the grasses in the play-scheme.
I'd find what else its first habitants have left:
a breeze-block ruin some scientist called home;
the Portaloos of vulcanologists;
spend Surtsian nights far from the red-shift
of streetlight, knowing it still exists

on the edge of memory. The cameras
have gone. I used to kid myself on cold
evenings walking home from school, and wonder
in the quiet after such a difficult birth;
the cries of sea-birds leaving me old
beyond my years in the youngest place on earth.

FROM

Tramp in Flames

(2006)

The Front

It stood firm for a fortnight, a cloud coast
that marked the front. All along the west
it towered; a full pan from north to south
held it in view. We watched it from the beach
each day for signs of movement. It didn't budge.
I thought of a tidal wave, freeze-framed,
but didn't say. Somebody on the third night
described it as a parting of the Red Sea
and then I couldn't help but squint for seals
or fish caught in its watery updraft,
but saw nothing. At certain times of day
you would have sworn you looked upon a land mass
with terns and gannets nested in its darkness.
Once, it grew the grey lip of a carrier deck.
Sunsets came a few degrees early
and, backlit, it glowed like something molten,
the birds heading for home crossing its lid
like car adverts with the sound turned down.
A two-week high of learning to live with it,
of tuning into paperbacks and rock pools;
the way the thrill of snow-capped peaks in summer
will slowly thaw, become invisible
and be just *there*: so it was with the front.
On the last day we woke to rain as thick
as diesel slicking the windows, all the shadows
scattered, the light turned low. We were inside it.

The Lapse

When the cutting edge was a sleight, a trick of time,
we blinked our way through *Jason and the Argonauts*,
thrilled by the stop-motion universe,
its brazen Talos grinding like a Dock Road crane,
and the Hydra's teeth sown into studio soil
by Harryhausen, who got between the frames
like a man who comes in bone dry from a downpour
by stopping the world and snapping out a path
through glassy rods right up to his front door.

Something as simple as Edgerton's milk splash
stilled to an ivory coronet would do it,
keep us quiet for hours as we learned to understand
the howling gale we stood in. Chilled to the core
we gasped as Ursula Andress stepped from the flame
and the unseen British-Pathé make-up department
took down her face, applying gravity with a trowel.
And I'd have to say something was taken from us.

On the dead sheep's seconds-long journey to nothing
with maggots working like a ball of fire,
every now and then a long bone settled awkwardly
like a break in continuity. Like an afternoon
of finding out for ourselves what death smelt like.
Long afternoons. Lying on our backs watching clouds
with the slow Doppler of a plane being bowed across the sky.
Give us back the giant day. Give us back what's ours.

Liverpool Disappears for a Billionth of a Second

Shorter than the blink inside a blink
the National Grid will sometimes make, when you'll
turn to a room and say: *Was that just me?*

People sitting down for dinner don't feel
their chairs taken away/put back again
much faster than that trick with tablecloths.

A train entering the Olive Mount cutting
shudders, but not a single passenger
complains when it pulls in almost on time.

The birds feel it, though, and if you see
starlings in shoal, seagulls abandoning
cathedral ledges, or a mob of pigeons

lifting from a square as at gunfire,
be warned, it may be happening, but then
those sensitive to bat-squeak in the backs

of necks, who claim to hear the distant roar
of comets on the turn – these may well smile
at a world restored, in one piece; though each place

where mineral Liverpool goes wouldn't believe
what hit it: all that sandstone out to sea
or meshed into the quarters of Cologne.

I've felt it a few times when I've gone home,
if anything, more often now I'm old,
and the gaps between get shorter all the time.

The Newsagent

My clock has gone although the sun has yet to take the sky.
I thought I was the first to see the snow, but his old eyes
have marked it all before I catch him in his column of light:
a rolled up metal shutter-blind, a paper bale held tight

between his knees so he can bring his blade up through the twine,
and through his little sacrifice he frees the day's headlines:
its strikes and wars, the weather's big seize up, runs on the pound.
One final star still burns above my head without a sound

as I set off. The dark country I grew up in has gone.
Ten thousand unseen dawns will settle softly on this one.
But with the streets all hushed I take the papers on my round
into the gathering blue, wearing my luminous armband.

Brutalist

Try living in one. Hang washing out to dry
and break its clean lines with your duds and smalls.
Spray tribal names across its subway walls
and crack its flagstones so the weeds can try

their damnedest. That's the way. Fly-tip the lives
you led, out past its edge, on the back field;
sideboards and mangles made sense in the peeled
spud light of the old house but the knives

are out for them now. This cellarless, unatticked
place will shake the rentman off, will throw
open its arms and welcome the White Arrow
delivery fleet which brings the things on tick

from the slush piles of the seasonal catalogues.
The quilt boxes will take up residence
on the tops of white wardrobes, an ambulance
raise blinds, a whole geography of dogs

will make their presence felt. And once a year
on Le Corbusier's birthday, the sun will set
bang on the pre-ordained exact spot
and that is why we put that slab just there.

One by one the shopkeepers will shut
their doors for good. A newsagent will draw
the line at buttered steps. The final straw
will fill the fields beyond. Now live in it.

As the Crow Flies

Became an idea, a pure abstraction,
all black vector, a distance in air miles;
Watling Street on the wing, a one-track mind
hell bent against a white, wintering sky.

Civic

Somebody should write on the paranoia of pines
   I wonder, making my way down to the shore
      of the reservoir in the dark,
         ignoring the signs
      which warn of deep water;
   there's a spring underfoot made up
of a billion needles and cones that carpet the floor

and a criss-cross of roots that keep the earth in its place
   and so the water clear: I've read the reports
      of the city engineers, done my homework,
         and move through the woods
      warily, the canopy high above
   whispering, watching (though I'm about as far
from another human being as it's possible to get here,

from our cities where you're never more than a few feet
   from a rat; where cameras comb the streets
      all hours), looking over my shoulder
         and seeing myself
      like that footage of sasquatch;
   or the private eye in *Chinatown*, hired
in a drought to find out what's happened to all the water

when all at once it's before me, a great glassy sheet,
   dark trees and hillsides held upside down
      in starlight: I've found Manchester
         at source, in the blues
      of a bathymetric map, in the clean
   and still repose before the nightmare of taps
and kettles. I scoop a cold handful up to my mouth

and taste the great nothing that comes before pipes
   pass on their trace of lead, before fonts
      leech their peck of limestone,
         before public baths
      annihilate with chlorine.
   The mind, honeycombed with aqueducts,
laps on the walls of Nineveh or Imperial Rome

but this is where it begins, if we can describe
   water in such terms, with middles and ends.
         I can hear the sluices – sound
         carries at this hour –
      and the start of the journey
   down, to the distant city, a steady roar
acting as water's own bar pilot, river guide, exit sign

and gravity holds open the door onto a man-made dark,
    culverts at first, and then the all-enclosing
        mysteries of pipe-work;
            a gentle incline
        and two-miles-per-hour
    average flow through the fell, blind
though sometimes proud when bridging a beck or ghyll

aloofly, sealed in concrete, on official council business.
    Two miles per hour; a hundred miles,
        so by my reckoning it'll take
            just over two days:
        if there was anybody else
    up here with me, I'd suggest 'Pooh sticks'
played out on a glacial, OS Pathfinder scale

or introduce those bright dyes I've seen used in the field
    in this very catchment area, turning streams
        a turbulent day-glo in a matter
            of stop-watched minutes;
        then catch a bus or train in my own time
    down to the city, and wait in the Albert Square
for the fountain to run orangeade, cream soda or dandelion-

and-burdock. You could walk: no Roman would have given
  a second thought to the hike, no Romantic neither.
    But this is water's pause for reflection.
      This is its downtime.
    Water seeking asylum
  lying low for a while, taking a chance
to gather its thoughts. Years ago, in the Liverpool Aquarium,

I read how the lungfish would dig into the parched
  riverbed, curl into a ball, secrete
    mucus, and generally do
      what it needed to
    to weather a spell between
  broad sheets of sudden rainfall that fell
weeks or months or years apart, wrapped up in itself;

though there was no word next to the tank on how water too
  needs to introspect, to find some high cistern
    or a road's camber after a storm
      that can hold a moon;
    those baths you see in fields
  plumbed into whitethorn, where the Green Man
might take his murky ablutions before going to ground

are favourites too. Wind from out of nowhere disturbs
    the signal. Some of these trees are mobile masts
        disguised as trees, I'm told, and this
            lake a reservoir
        disguised as a lake. It looks
    the part alright; in fact, has already starred
in films as body double to Como and Geneva

though it knows it's an offcomer, a baby in glacial terms,
    and nothing much has pooled and stuck.
        There's no host of golden daffodils, no
            Bluebird going down
        in black-and-white to rise
    again in colour, no Post Office Tower
leant like a dipstick to illustrate its unnatural fathoms,

just those rumours that seem to follow reservoirs around:
    a drowned village, church bells on rough nights,
        the souls who stood their ground
            calling from the depths,
        that kind of thing. Then a blackbird
    breaks cover, and its cries manage to sound
genuinely bereft for lost acres of thicket and undergrowth

and miles of hedgerow. A Water Board van snakes its way
    silently northwards up the A591
        along the opposite bank,
            and it's getting light
        so I step back into the trees
    not wanting to be seen by anyone.
In this poem disguised as a meditation on water

it's now as good a time as any to tell you, reader,
    how I've driven up to this spot in a hire car
        and stand at the water's edge
            drawn by a keen sense
        of civic duty: I plan to break
    the great stillness and surface of this lake-
cum-reservoir by peeing quietly into the supply

and no harm will come to anything or anyone. Consider
    this: no shoal will surface out of sync
        like driftwood; no citizens
            will draw a cold draught
        of LSD, or run a hot bath
    of nerve agent in two days' time. This act
is so small it will only really occur in the mind's eye

and those particles – smaller than rods and cones – that escape
the filters and treatment plant won't register
in any sense. And so my ripples
head for God-knows-where
as light strengthens by increment
and a tree falls in the woods and no one hears,
though I can't swear to any of this: I wasn't here.

Somebody else packed up in a hurry, walked back
up a slope, bastard tricky with roots, came to
the quiet road in the green shade
that leads round the lake;
passed a city's coat of arms
and some Latin he couldn't read, looked out
from a wall across a body of water at chest height

and gasped at the thought of the pressure, the pounds-per-brick,
and felt alone up there then, and wanted to drive
far away from those high offices,
from the danger signs
where water stands in the hills
with the eyes, from the man-made distances
that have haunted his ears; from the paranoia of pines.

Duel

Split pistols on a woodchip wall a decade,
faked alloys, brandished, facing one another
above a brick fireplace (another bullshitter –

ersatz and cold). These two bisected bastards
were only half there, but they stared me down.
The horse brasses and Spanish fans were harmless

but guns form in the womb. If my dad was out,
bored, I'd take up arms and clasp each half
together, then I'd pick a photograph

along the mantelpiece, and draw a bead
between the eyes of some ancestral second;
or (this was harder) turn the pistol on

myself. I'd hold its shape along the midline
by sucking the muzzle – it tasted of television –
and use my thumbs to blow my fucking brains out.

Tramp in Flames

Some similes act like heat shields for re-entry
to reality: a tramp in flames on the floor.
We can say *Flame on!* to invoke the Human Torch
from the Fantastic Four. We can switch to art
and imagine Dali at this latitude
doing CCTV surrealism.
We could compare him to a protest monk
sat up the way he is. We could force the lock
of memory: at the crematorium
my uncle said the burning bodies rose
like Draculas from their boxes.
                                                        But his layers
burn brightly, and the salts locked in his hems
give off the colours of a Roman candle,
and the smell is like a foot-and-mouth pyre
in the middle of the city he was born in,
and the bin bags melt and fuse him to the pavement
and a pool forms like the way he wet himself
sat on the school floor forty years before,
and then the hand goes up. *The hand goes up.*

Johnny Thunders Said

You can't put your arms around a memory.
The skin you scuffed climbing the black railings
of school, the fingertips that learned to grip
the pen, the lips that took that first kiss
are gone, my friend. Nothing has stayed the same.
The brain? A stockpot full of fats and proteins
topped up over a fire stoked and tended
a few decades. Only the bones endure,
stilt-walking through a warm blizzard of flesh,
making sure the whole thing hangs together,
our lifetimes clinging on as snow will lag
bare branches, magnifying them mindlessly.
Dear heart, you've put a brave face on it, but know
exactly where the hugs and handshakes go.

Requiem for a Friend

after Rainer Maria Rilke

My dead are doing fine and are at home
wandering off the street into a night class
or half-lit drinking school among their own,
glad to be out of it. But since you've gone
on ahead – forgive the spatial shorthand,
it's all that works in this world – I've been troubled
by little things: a polystyrene cup
edging across a table on the train
like contact at a séance; a squirrel who stops
and eyes me sadly through the kitchen window;
opposites of portents, things that have me stand
to damp a past soon as I feel it build.
  This is a worry. I never had you down
as someone who'd stray back, being the sort
on even terms with the dead, and never one
for doing things by half; lighting your breath
on overproof rum, and other party tricks
for sure, but mostly your approach to the art
convinced me that you'd fit right in 'out there';
so why is it when a radiator knocks
I think of you as frightened? They say Death
requires that those left behind secure
their minds, and can arrange a late-night visit
for an audience of one; others go looking
and tune in to a mighty passing trade;

and the medium of the page is close to hand,
but until the words choose me I'm left with things
going bump: and these all say you want back in.
The opposite – again – of birds that board
a tube carriage for crumbs, but just as afraid
on the journey between stops. Is this what friends
are for: to say the door is always open?
Heart on the latch, I lie awake and listen.
Classic haunts demand some bricks and mortar
and yours are London stock. Their soot-caked yellow
constructs a meeting place on every corner
and draughty rooms you read your poems in,
though the herringbone tweed you wore each winter
disturbs the steady signal of the pointing
so sightings have been abundant – across streets
I've watched you blur into shopfronts and windows –
and now even the tolling of a skip
being filled, or a door slam in the downstairs flat
are noises off, a loud prompt from the wings;
they run a thumbnail down the cellophane
sleep wraps me in, and strip it. So. What's up?

Instead of begging at the station mouth
are you trying to press the all-zones travel pass
of night into my palm? Should I explore
a city just a few shades out of whack
from this, built in its shadows of slant rain?

Then I'll enter into it: I'll climb its stairwells,
its steps that won't add up; I'll stand for hours
and learn to make myself invisible
as its buskers do; I'll walk from north to south

approaching all its Big Issue vendors
on their blind sides; I'll mark the surfaces
where women straighten hair and fix their lipstick,
sift through an Oxfam shop's doorway moraine;
paused on the threshold of a tattoo parlour
I'll be in two minds – neither one thing nor the other –
and down one street I'll find a taxidermist
who deals in urban fauna, mesmerised
by a fox's backward glance, a pigeon's arabesque,
a feral cat's gelled hackles. This city casts
strange shadows and is full of trapped light, closed
out back in meat safes, stockrooms, nurseries,
the curtained blood glow of insomniacs,
of penlights shone into a captive's mouth,
of hands placed over torches deep inside
a cave system, of faces turned to masks.
I'll leave before that moment loved by guides
the world under: *Now turn your torches off*.

If there was one thing you knew inside out
it was illusionism, the ticket hall
of mirrors, and we were taken for a ride
as willing passengers along a strong-line
not found on Beck's map or The Great Bear,
barely skimming the surface, then rattling down
to coalmine depths. Dropping your knife or fork
you'd frown skywards as if the object fell
from some great height. It had: Washington Square
in the rain, where you'd watched Robert Lowell's quart
of liquor shatter when his brown bag broke
and he looked up to heaven or low cloud.

To prove there were a downside to each joke
the ground gives way if someone tries this now.
   It seems there was a world before I knew you,
a world I was at large in, but back then
its plate glass and its mirrors just confused
or startled me with angry slaps of sun.
You showed me how to move about this stage,
so why now are you banging into things
and throwing your weight around? Did you leave clues
strewn like flowers up to your final afternoon?
Should I have seen or read an evil omen,
in a house whose front and back doors had blown open,
an unexpected bar of small-hours birdsong,
or breaking news of flash floods through a village?
   Slip into the light. See if I'm afraid
to look you in the face. When the dead return
they've every right to step out from the shadows
and harden once more in our field of vision.
   Slip into an element more visible
as someone moving through the dark will trip
a lamp sensor outside and flood the garden
with halogen, a false dawn for the rose
and December moth, which comes to light – but real
enough for a few seconds – so a shade
can stand before us plain as day, even though
we know its sun lies deep in the horizon.

It takes a while to grasp but I think I know
the worst: sometimes I have you waking up
inside a funhouse room, the ceiling trying

to rain above the mosh-pit of your bed,
and as the paper peels in long sad scrolls,
you inch your way as firemen feel ahead
using their knuckles down a smoke-filled hall
(because a hand that feels its way palmwards,
if shocked, can trip and grab live wiring),
finding a snow globe boiled dry, a mirror
blackened and cracked, the brickwork kiln-hot,
and sometimes pass, eyes streaming, into chambers
of utter loss, carbon-encrusted dark
like houses where the roof has gone, from childhood,
abandoned to what wind blows through. In short
you find a place of pure aphelion.
You let the night get in; invited it.
Just shadow by shadow at first, as bar room smoke
entered the exoskeleton of your coat
and found a home there with the poisonous looks
and sly remarks absorbed, the ones you never
reflected back, with interest. Lifting it
onto its peg, I have you frisk its warmth
and deep inside its bottomless pockets
winkle what feel like seeds along its hems.
Gallstones, fulgurites – but still you pick the fluff
from them like ancient mints and are surprised,
alone there at the end of some lost night,
to find some trace of sweetness has survived.
Inside your senses you were sweet enough.

Time to lament. Your cometary blood
lost track; the circuit broke; how could it know

its point-of-no-return was being crossed?
A stanza-break can stand between two seasons
but blood is curious and your blood rushed
amazed into a room it never knew,
escaping from its greater circulation.
This party was worth crashing. If you could
you'd always stuff your pockets, weigh up ashtrays,
and stretch the hospitality to its limits;
your blood was no different. Ill-bred, it flung
itself through halls of everything you'd thought,
a slow stain on a scan but from the ground
perfect cathedrals, chambers of errors.
Trouble was, such sightseeing leads down slipways
that take you into Time, and Time is long,
and Time runs down, and Time slams all the doors,
and Time is like a medium's lapse in recall . . .
   Your leaving as the days began to shorten
has left me wondering if the hours you spent
back here sent leader shoots, mycelial
pathways into your futures, as we all
could go so many ways each given moment.
And if one message came back through the drowned
Bronx subways, or the scorched earth of North London,
meaning you knew, or knew as threads in soil
weave through the dark, build instinct in the hope
of being heard before the nights draw in.
   (Nothing. No spinal shiver. No failing light
the moment you sat bolt upright in bed
and called out, isolated as a sea stack.
No boom of blood like waves crashing inside

a cellar. All the skilled, frantic attentions
around you didn't register. As wars
and weather systems do their worst, as seabirds
must wheel now at the world's edge, others sleep.
Until bad news comes falling from the heights
of column inch or midnight call, we walk
the same old world, even as each distant landslide
re-writes the coves and inlets of its shores.)

And so you died and were put out to sea
from a neuro ward early on a Thursday evening,
lights coming on as nurses snipped you free
of oxygen mask, wires, indwelling needles,
the night schools silent for summer re-opening,
their door bolts scraping through old ruts and puddles.

Once there'd have been a right to-do: coloraturas
on wax cylinders; daguerreotypes; death masks,
where now we all observe small silences
or fail to rise to feature desks' requests.
The high styles have all gone or been disowned.
Could this be why you've come back: to flesh out
the bone-clack of lament? Can you hear me?
I'd like to spray my voice out like a mist net
over the slivers of your death, and rag
my range – from shout to whisper – down to tatters
so all my words would have to go round bare-arsed
and shivering in the snarls of that torn voice.
Lament never being enough, I'll point the finger:
no one person withdrew you from your tasks
(and anyway, he's everywhere and nowhere)
but I accuse him: you know who you are.

Whenever, walking through the day, I'm mugged
by some transporting detail – say the sound
of rain feeding a puddle on the platform
from one cracked pane a hundred feet above me –
then I don't want to know. I'd sooner warm
to a galaxy of pigeon shit than dwell
on ideas of angels crying in anger.

All this suffering has lasted far too long,
we can't bear it: it's grown too big to handle,
a generator of mechanical love
which runs itself and barks up trade and makes
a profit out of showing us our loss.
Who really has a right to their possessions?
And how can any of us hold onto things
that cannot hold their own selves; who can catch
themselves whole, as they glance past their reflections?
That childhood trick is gone. No more than divers
can grasp the light that leads them onto wrecks,
nor any of the bright groupers or wrasse
survive the sudden bends back to the surface,
the tonnes of air; so we can't call back one
who, unaware of us now, moves along
a narrow beam of single thought and faith
that keeps the great night out, that sees him safest:
unless we have a calling to do wrong.

Because this is wrong, if anything is wrong:
not to unlock the freedom of a love
with all the inner freedom we can summon.
In love, you only need respect one truth:

let go. Any infant's finger-grip will prove
how holding on comes easy. We must unlearn it.

You're not still here? Still hiding in some corner?
Nothing you didn't know already, I learned it
mostly from you. You seemed to pass through days
wide open, opposite to shade. First light
on Green Lanes. Love is walking home alone
and art is one long runner, an escape
in nothing like real time: both courses meet
and this is where you live, an attitude
that will outlast the big dune shifts, the minor
aftershocks. You'd already withdrawn
beyond us all, slipped out the back, split early
before the slow dance and the house lights up,
into the ashen dawn of your sixth decade,
leaving the customary great unfinished
poem: the one that has to stay unfinished.

If you are still here, moving through the darkness,
if my voice has found a sympathetic resonance
and solid things are stirred on shallow sound waves,
then hear me out, and help me out. It's easy
to slip and lose our balance, and it's *back*
to your post and *look busy* and *here's your desk*.
One day, just sat there staring at my hands,
a pulsing in their vein-work broke a spell
just for a dreamlike moment. It happens: blood
reminding blood. And anyone who heaves
their own will know, the law of gravity
can pull it back to weight and worthlessness.

Between our little lives and the great work
there is bad blood, pent up, an ancient feud.
You'll understand if anybody will.

But don't come back. If you can stand it, stay
dead with the dead. The dead have their own tasks.
But help me, in your own time, in your own way,
as far-off things can help us: deep within.

Filler

This doodle darkening my delegate pack
   on the sixth day of a seven-day conference
is keeping me from screaming. I have this knack
   for honeycombing out the present. Once
I didn't, and the world would turn to filler.
      Not hardnosed economics, like the soldier
      being sent up to the front, or why our butcher
   saw fit to scoop sawdust into his mince.

Neither makeweight nor object from the past
   sticking it out from surplus-to-requirements
to value; time sanctifying waste.
   Not superstitious acres farmers grant
      to their crop devil, or a brewer's angels' share.
For me, none of this was strictly filler.
      I saw the use in test-cards and screen-savers.
   Even *Farley, get in goal!* bore fruitful stints.

But never listening to Horace, nor my mother,
eternity turned everything to filler,
our landscapes ground in time to a fine powder,
the bones of Stone Age man, readers and writers,
   the great iron ships, the balance sheets, the sales spikes,
         the last plant standing ancient history,
a sun like blood. Next thing, I'm waving *Goodbye!*
to the hydrogen atom as the seas boil dry,
      which is no way to live. So I take shelter
in the moment's coral, careful not to look
   into the whirlpool of the conference clock.

Whitebeam

The sixty-miles-per-hour plants, the growth
that lines the summer corridors of sight
along our major roads, the overlooked
backdrop to 'Preston, 37 miles'.
Speed-camera foliage; the white flowers
of Mays and Junes, the scarlet fruits of autumn
lay wasted in the getting from A to B.
Hymn to forward-thinking planting schemes,
though some seem in two minds: the greenwood leaves
are white-furred, have a downy underside
as if the heartwood knew in its heart of hearts
the days among beech and oak would lead to these
single file times, these hard postings,
and civilised itself with handkerchiefs.

The Heron

One of the most begrudging avian take-offs
is the heron's *fucking hell, all right, all right,*
I'll go the garage for your flaming fags
cranky departure, though once they're up
their flight can be extravagant. I watched
one big spender climb the thermal staircase,
a calorific waterspout of frogs
and sticklebacks, the undercarriage down
and trailing. Seen from antiquity
you gain the Icarus thing; seen from my childhood
that cursing man sets out for Superkings,
though the heron cares for neither as it struggles
into its wings then soars sunwards and throws
its huge overcoat across the earth.

A God

A god who checks you've turned the oven off
in some unnumbered radio galaxy
never sleeps or swerves from His one duty.
You never know: in the middle of the night
you could be up putting a pizza in,
and what does He care? It's the Middle Ages

where He lives. Watching over your stove
beats anything closer to hand: in two places
at once, He'd rather listen to the ticks
of the oven preheating than sit through jousts
or another spit roast. He enjoys the rings
glowing concentrically in your dark kitchen;

planetary, He thinks. Music of the spheres.
Hell, in his pianoless world, what He'd give
to stand before it like an instrument
and set its greasy dials for the hearts of suns,
careful not to raise the number of the beast
on its console – that would be a mistake –

but play all night bathed in its infra-reds;
electric music (the god of hearth
is banging from His sealed-up chimney breast),
ammonia, wire wool, black residue
on the brain pan, the upright honky-tonk
of metals cooling down when morning comes.

The Scarecrow Wears a Wire

The scarecrow wears a wire in the top field.
At sundown, the audiophilic farmer
who bugged his pasture unpicks the concealed
mics from its lapels. He's by the fire

later, listening back to the great day,
though to the untrained ear there's nothing much
doing: a booming breeze, a wasp or bee
trying its empty button-hole, a stitch

of wrensong now and then. But he listens late
and nods off to the creak of the spinal pole
and the rumble of his tractor pulling beets
in the bottom field, which cuts out. In a while

somebody will approach over ploughed earth
in caked Frankenstein boots. There'll be a noise
of tearing, and he'll flap awake by a hearth
grown cold, waking the house with broken cries.

The Westbourne at Sloane Square

You again! Of all the bomb-scarred stonework
and air vents underfoot I knew by heart.
You, still going strong in your black pipe
above the passengers and mice-live tracks.
You, flowing through eighteenth-century parkscape
into an ironclad late-Victorian night.

Pissed and standing on the eastbound platform
I was a tin soldier who'd fallen in
to London's storm drain, sent spinning around
the Circle Line long after closing time,
and all along I've carried these trapped sounds
I hear again and recognise deep down.

How many miles of shit have you crawled through
since we last met? I'd do it all again.
We've less choice than we think, the likes of you and me.
Blind water, borne along or bearing through,
escaping in a hurry for open sea.
To think we start as innocent as rain.

FROM
The Dark Film
(2012)

The Power

Forget all of that end-of-the-pier
palm-reading stuff. Picture a seaside town
in your head. Start from its salt-wrack-rotten smells
and raise the lid of the world to change the light,
then go as far as you want: the ornament
of a promenade, the brilliant greys of gulls,
the weak grip of a crane in the arcades
you've built, ballrooms to come alive at night,
then a million-starling roost, an opulent
crumbling like cake icing . . .
                                        Now, bring it down
in the kind of fire that flows along ceilings,
that knows the spectral blues; that always starts
in donut fryers or boardwalk kindling
in the dead hour before dawn, that leaves pilings
marooned by mindless tides, that sends a plume
of black smoke high enough to stain the halls
of clouds. Now look around your tiny room
and tell me that you haven't got the power.

Adults

I'd look up to them looming on street corners,
or down on them at night through my bedroom blinds,
crashing home from the Labour Club, mad drunk.
After a while I decided they must be unhappy.

And this didn't tally at all with my view of their world.
Adults could float through days sole sovereigns
of everything around them, could pass through walls
of childish silence, or just take off in the *Sunbeam*.

So why did I find them at hometime slumped in their chairs
or throwing their tea up the wall? Why did they cry
on their own downstairs with the whole house listening in
or plead softly to people who weren't even there?

You think you know all the answers at that age.
You can't wait to grow up and sort them out, then go
to live in Mayfair or Singapore, wear a smoking jacket
and drink gin slings all day, like real writers do.

Quality Street

How many other kids would turn
   themselves into a camera
replete with scrims and gels and tints
   to see the world in new colours?
Soul billows through net curtains.
   A glutton finds his favourite seat
and sets to working through a tin of Quality Street.

The wrapper of a strawberry cream
   unpeels a vivid red to dye
the evening bloody monochrome.
   Under a pre-Cambrian sky
the scale of blood and blood-shadow has made
   an ancient fortress of the maisonettes;
a dog crossing the square is flayed
      alive, leaves bloody tracks
and looks back with a blood-bright eye
   before it finds a bin-shed door
and roots the opened guts of bin liners,
   all in the light of a great fire,
and when our sun becomes a swollen core
there will be other evenings like this to endure.

But this is now, or rather, then. The gold
is taken from a toffee penny and held
   over the eyes: gold cellophane
   that makes a legend of the rain,

a sheet so small being beaten out
by greedy vision until the whole estate
turns lustrous from the eye's electroplate.

Blue next, from a coconut macaroon,
the day-for-night
filter you might
look through to turn a sun into a moon.
That dog's a Quink hound now; the swing park is a ruin;
the shrubs outside The Highwayman
scratch up against the galleon
pub-sign that's swinging in a wind
straight out of Queen Anne's England,
and there's a general deepening, a thousand shades
cast by the washing on the lines
that tacks hard like a navy in full sail.

Lee, Wranglers, Fruit of the Loom
restored to virginal denim,
and midges in a streetlamp's glow
are swirling like marine snow
at depths where light isn't supposed to go.
But too much blue is bad: it suffocates
the senses to spend all your time
in this sliver of the spectrum;
and blue is precincts of celestial fate,
the concrete present flooded by eternal weight.

Adding a yellow wrapper to
the sheet of blue
creates a green which covers everything,

a thousand years of growth at once,
our steady state, if given half a chance,
and you can hear birds sing.
Empire of moss and long barrow,
each doorway is an earth entrance
to *long ago* and *ever since,*
a source, Eurydice's hatch, a mammal burrow
that slows the eye and leads us down
into a sump where we could drown
happily, in a medium we've never known:
the future yet to rain, the past long flown.
But winter comes back harder, flesh falls from the bones

of trees whose flooded nests hang plain,
this novelty of looking drained
away, and which of us could say:
To morrow do thy worst, for I have liv'd to day . . .
Quinoline Yellow, beta-carotene,
Allura Red, riboflavin, tartrazine,
you took us out of time and gave us power
to hype the moment, dye the day, and rob the hour.

The Airbrake People

You could drive a bus between each lonely gasp.
I listened through the night for steam-powered calls
between civic twilights, between songbirds,
a silence shared with shouts and breaking glass.

I pictured them as birds for a long time,
shy, cuspate creatures with the eyes of snakes
that haunted reed and marsh, ancient as light in the east,
at dusk coming among our streets and houses

the way an eddy of wind would worry the empties
and find a note so low it turned your bones
to milk. I'd count the minutes between each hiss:
all exhalation, nothing but dying fall

as if the night itself received a puncture,
as if there were a wounding in the dark.
They spoke to me. Or spoke to something in me.
And that's when I decided they were people,

a lost tribe come right to the edge of their woods.
I'd found signs in the bus stand and the car parks:
the funerary spoors of emptied ashtrays,
their hairclips and their little broken combs.

And none of this seemed stranger to me then than
finding ploughs or hunters in the sky,
or seeing Jack Frost in his suit of lights.
Something in me knew they were cold and starved.

One by one they were entering our clearing,
our blood-orange streetlight, our muddied dark,
so they could release those long, pneumatic sighs,
and that was how the airbrake people died.

Google Earth

Now I'm a hand setting the globe to spin,
finding a country, starting to zoom in
now I'm an eye. Now I'm a meteorite.

The scars of business corridors, the white
clay works, national parkland, estuaries.
A refinery built from Camemberts and Bries!

Now I'm a hand again, steadying my fall,
steering by starlight on the ground, black holes
of reservoirs, flight paths of major roads.

Now I'm an eye and there are never clouds
because the west wind of the Internet
blows silently down lost bus routes, birth streets,

the school roof still in bad need of repair,
the swing park all deserted at this hour,
which is no-hour. Now I'm the midnight sun

lighting the places where we've been and gone.
The ground comes up. A field sharpens to grain.
The trees screw into leaf. Now I'm a drop of rain.

Now I'm a balloon by Odilon Redon.
And now my chute snags up on power-lines.
If we looked outside, eyeballs might block the sun.

Even above the lake isles of Lough Gill,
Adlestrop's dismantled barrow, a hill
on the road north of Poughkeepsie, there are eyes

now all the world's a drop zone of the mind.

The Spoiler

The Spoiler wouldn't ever
reveal its ends to me.
Would never speak of rivers
flowing into the sea

or let slip how the boy
would get the girl. It said
that I should look away,
or cover my ears instead.

But then The Spoiler peeled
its gloves off, and I felt
the rough skin of the world
those silky hands had built.

The Cellar

Mind your head. The ceiling is low.
Slowly down the gritty steps
into the slower air of the cellar
past a ledge of tools and tins
of paint whose colours could be matched
upstairs, raised in a nick or scratch.

Following days of heavy rain
a chronic puddle reoccurs.
Its flagstones form a last attempt
at civilization. No coal comes now
but enough has fallen through this hole
to power the boilers of a ship.

The dark and damp stay anchored here
but fire once shared the room upstairs
with television. The utter disdain
the cellar must have felt for a world
where Callas' earring or Ringo's snare
would catch the studio lights and flare

jet black across an ocean. Here,
a fathom below the floorboards,
in an agony of hooks and nails,
the colours peter out and stone
begins. Cobble and clay. Hard pan.
Below doesn't bear thinking about.

Moles

Within sight of the blue of the sky,
with meadow scents and the song of birds
as the gradient slackened, he looked back to find
more emptiness than he thought this earth

could hold. In this version of the myth
we leave him there, helpless and blind,
skimming for worms in the topsoil, cursed
with shovels that can't even hold a lyre.

Pop

Just as Beau Brummell's ferrule
and waistcoat have merged
with the wigs and stay-laces
of five decades earlier

in my mind, so the Ted
and the Mod and the Rocker
will slowly converge
in the fullness of time

to a mixture, an aggregate
post-war character
dug from a beach that
was once five miles inland,

the salt dark dissolving
the edges, the features,
till they can't tell between us
and none of it matters.

Cyan

I'm one of those model men
in barbershop or unisex
salon windows. I've held my breath
here, like this, for decades.

O distant youth, O brilliantine,
I saw myself the other day
across the street in running time:
gabardined, red-faced, gone grey.

The cow's-lick and the kiss curl.
I'm holding out. I'm blue in the face.
Telstar still orbits the Earth.
We don't like what you've done to the place.

The Note Produced

The sixty-four-foot organ pipe,
the low C, shuddering *Jesus Christ*,
the engine room that makes cathedrals
dive, dive, dive, fathoms of flue

that drill into the bedrock, shift
knuckles and long bones in the crypt,

and you can feel the bottom line
right where the ribs all congregate,
a shiver trapped and brought to life.

The Dark Film

The dark film goes on general release.
Floodlights rake the low cloud base
above the scratchy London planes
and iron palings of Leicester Square.

Unrated dark, two hours long.
We wonder where the film was shot:
the *Night Mail* stopped, or *Empire State*
caught midway through a power cut,

or if they'd left the lens cap on
and gone with it, declared it 'art',
or if this were a film at all
or leader-tape blocking the light.

But something happens to the print
the further on into its run,
the further out each reel is sent:
audiences start seeing things.

An eyelash in Hitchin's Regal
grows four foot long, electrified,
a hairspring from a town-hall clock
in the screen's top right hand side

and in the Brighton Hippodrome
a pair of tracks cut by a bad
projector somewhere on the road
from Soho leaves them mesmerised

and by the time the film has reached
the oilrigs and the inset isles
it crackles like a bonfire
and radiant fibres twitch and turn

to thistledown and stars, scratches
to flak, to Dolby bumps felt in
the gut, a tracer fire of dust,
then faces, looked at long enough.

Odometer

Whatever way the tale is told –

– it always ends with a new owner
screwing open the odometer
all keen for winding back the clock
and finding there a folded note
which reads: *Oh no. Please. Not again.*
Or something else along those lines.

The surgeon lifts a heart from ice.
In the heat of his hands it begins to purr
like a bat being brought from a house at dusk,
and the way I always tell it, whoever
receives the heart feels ten years younger.
They only remember a blinding light

and a joke they must have heard when they were under.

Outside Cow Ark

Is mine the only heart out in this weather?
No. Grouse hearts beat in that turning heather.
Those midges scribbling patterns in late sun
fill their wings by dint of pinprick organs.
The privatized stream where I parked the car
contains trout hearts, idling in dead water.

Mine was switched on in another century,
in coal-fired rooms. Now other circuitry
that came online under this April's moon,
or cold hatches that sparked this very dawn,
is tuning one by one into my ancient valves.
The cardiac amperage hearts keep to themselves

links me up with livestock in the fold
but wilder blood-pumps out there must behold
a strange contraption, built for a long haul
far and away from home. The grouse will fall
before the year is done; the fish short out
inside a greater current; flies won't last the night.

Nostalgie Concrète

I'm ageing at the same increasing rate
but the years have bottled it, turned on their heels.
You've seen those films where pools come to the boil
then turn to glass as divers zip them shut,
feet first all the way back to the springboard;
you've seen Lancashire chimneys rise like trunks
of brick-dust mastodons, then stiffen up.
But living it? Listen. I'm one week in

and I never want to see a raindrop run
up a windowpane again, a biro drink
its words, or squatting dogs trained to insert
a link of turds. Eating out *is* eating out:
a string of unchewed bunting from the mouths
of people sobering up, re-entering coats
and leaving like an audience with the Queen
backwards into a night that's getting younger.

Though this isn't film. More the sun taking its light back,
coronal flares like bonfire sparks from each tree,
wall and face; more how mercury flows to the bright
elemental font. Looking back into that dark
I can see what's going to happen: friends go and come,
unsmoke more cigarettes and shed the pounds,
but mostly they'll forget. No one will see me
(each moment constantly undoes itself)

so I'll never meet them on the journey back
as they lose books, lighten up, and find the smiles
they didn't know they'd lost. And on the day
I die, an old ghost in 1971,
the sun will set in the east, the rain will rise
from pavements to the clouds, while all my friends
look through me with the wordless, wide-eyed stares
they were born with, as they head for home, feet first.

Creep

Shale rises a thousand feet
almost vertically; the sun
sets sometime shortly after noon.

Now the steam press of the cloud base
has put a tin lid on the day,

the lake darkening and darkening
as if a dye has been released

into us: toxin, tincture
crossing the blood–brain barrier,
the greyscale empire of slate.

But something else is happening
altogether vast and slow,

and as the light begins to go
we start to hear the scree, keeping
its stony, ancient time, ticking,

a kind of rock drizzle, the micro
readjustments of a clock

kept wound and running since the ice
retreated, and we feel the shock

of time in time, a pulse running
within the mainspring of a world
that keeps gaining and doesn't care.

Rapid Hardware

Seed and ore, onwards, towards
ruin and dross, and the hardware shop's

long pause, its hundred spirit levels
in stock, its silent lanes of timber,

its screw-drivers with long-shanks caught
in handles clear as Baltic amber,

its tacks and nails in swarm before
they leave to hold the world together,

its library of sandpaper
before it passes into scraps

and fragments, onwards, wrapped around
so many blocks of two-by-four;

and finding ourselves far from art
among these raw materials –

washers in the charity box,
unctions on high sunstruck shelves –

this is a proper place for prayer,
astringent turps and cross our hearts.

The Mind

Asleep, the organs form a line to see
the mind. The liver won't stand for much more,
so the mind issues a warning in the form
of a sad dream that will haunt it through the day.

The kidneys do their double-entry audit,
the same old calculations: the mind has heard it
ten thousand times, but feigns interest and calm.
This number crunching can't do any harm.

The spleen reminds the mind that in the death
it will stay open longest of them all,
remaining at its post, admitting cells
to a party gone cold, past each lung's last breath,

beyond the heart's much vaunted in-and-out.
But the mind reminds the spleen 'glorified pump'
is out-of-line; that it must learn to let
go of the heart's cruel 'overrated sump'.

Let go. Forgive. Fall into line. Move on.
The mind repeats itself. When all is said
and done, as the last gland shuffles out at dawn,
tired, the mind comes to the bit it dreads.

Cloaca Maxima

I

Sewer-jumping in a childhood twilight
the boy looks up a moment and feels something.
Water thick as Bovril doesn't move.
There's a holding of the breath in a concrete outfall.
It's an ear-to-the-rail moment,
or pipe-work, leading back to God-knows-where,
before an iron door slams shut on the splendours.

II

Moment containing all the fine escapees
of history, crawling through the dark, emerging
from unmarked graves aligned to navigations
they dug and died alongside. One long chain gang
raised from tobacco fields unlocked from work-songs
they sung in warmer, thicker air – *If you*
Don't believe I'm a sinkin, look what a hole I'm in –
the blistered of the Dismal Swamp Canal
who've travelled via the Underground Railroad
and Anacharsis Cloots – what's he doing here?
– with Representatives of the Human Race
all covered in shit, blinking in the light of day,
the shut-in, nameless multitudes, the lost bones,
the leg-irons and the long shanks and the ledger-
entered of Goree Island: all raised up!

III

Look at these three, marching through the visible field
from left to right, a ragged and sooty sentence
in the buttery, limestone light, in the middle of a century.
Marching into three futures long since past.

The little one says to the big one: *Who is this bloke?*
in a lost vernacular of Parisian sweeps
which the camera couldn't record. To which the big one
replies: *Never mind. Keep looking straight ahead*

though he's secretly intrigued. The apparatus
is a little like when a chimney grate's sealed off
by a canvas rig. And how many days has he seen
as a pinprick at the end of a carbon flue?

The middle one has climbed towards this light
so many times already in his short life,
and you want to tell him how long he's lasted in it
where so many others are shut in the dusty dark.

IV

Or think in terms of a movie shot
on a shoestring, where the eye is drawn
to the extras who are swapping hats
and passing by again and again.

Only replace its flimsy set
with sewers and ditches and holes in the ground,
and a scene that lasts millions of feet;
and the background babble with the sound

of a bullwhip that reverberates
down dark tunnels, and the same faces
come round eventually if you wait
for a few lifetimes and remain in your places.

V

The sleepers' hands are put to work.
Workhouse children unsnarl looms
and sharecroppers shuck peas from pods
and cocklers rake through dark mortar
and cotton pickers twist the buds
and bonded women solder boards
and run the fabric through the foot
and guide it down the miles of seam
and punkah wallahs pull the cord
and galley rowers bend through oars
and railroad workers tap the rails
and drainage diggers heft the spade
and all of this and so much more
is happening in the place of dreams.
The sleepers' hands are put to work.

VI

And this is what the boy has seen: the dreams
kept hidden, either by great distances
or the pearlescent blind eye that we need
to grow to keep the world under our noses
safely removed. The millions of mixed shades
are still running beneath our surfaces
and visible to those who just step sideways
anywhere: a city square at dusk,
a sun-warmed wall asking to have an ear
lent to its crumbling roughcast, old outfalls
like this one, where a boy gave way to thought
thirty years ago, on a backfield, in the north.

Big Fish

It's like returning to a natal pool
after years of doing business in great waters,
and only a few will make it whole,
the dreams of youth unsullied and intact
after all they've seen in the world's working mirrors,
its splendid distractions, the weight of its cold hard facts,

and the driver lets you off at the foot of the hill
and you pass the substation humming its old song
about power being stepped down, the climbing frame
in the swing-park posing its puzzle, and before long
your birth street greets you with an ambush of smells:
teatimes in doorways where no-one remembers your name.

The Circuit

I want to be laid to rest in a substation.
I want the padlocked door I tried for hours
as a bored and disrespectful child to be swung open;
to be placed respectfully next to transformers.

These will hum to me in the quiet after you've gone.
The gravel that my brick mausoleum stands in
is freshly raked, but soon teasels and docks
will grow waist high, and I want this to happen.

Lying in the dark river of flux
I want to feel the increased demand of autumn
in a frantic tittle-tattle of switching gear.
Between the power station and our home

I want to lie and abide and bridge the gap
so you might think of me as the days shorten;
a little shock each time you find you're sat
in the dark, and rise to put the big light on.

Index of Titles

Index of First Lines